Eating Bread and Honey

ALSO BY PATTIANN ROGERS

The Expectations of Light

The Tattooed Lady in the Garden

Legendary Performance

Splitting and Binding

Geocentric

Firekeeper: New and Selected Poems

Eating Bread and Honey

PATTIANN ROGERS

MILKWEED
EDITIONS

Published 1997 by Milkweed Editions
Printed in the United States of America
Cover design by Tara Christopherson, Fruitful Results Design
Cover art, "Air," by Georgette Sosin
Interior design by Will Powers
The text of this book is set in Legacy Serif.
97 98 99 00 01   5 4 3 2 1
First Edition

Milkweed Editions is a not-for-profit publisher.
We gratefully acknowledge support from the Elmer L. and Eleanor J. Andersen Foundation;
James Ford Bell Foundation; Target Stores, Dayton's, and Mervyn's by the Dayton Hudson
Foundation; Doherty, Rumble and Butler; General Mills Foundation; Honeywell Foundation;
Jerome Foundation; The McKnight Foundation; Andrew W. Mellon Foundation;
Minnesota State Arts Board through an appropriation by the Minnesota State Legislature;
Challenge and Literature Programs of the National Endowment for the Arts; Lawrence and
Elizabeth Ann O'Shaughnessy Charitable Income Trust in honor of Lawrence M.
O'Shaughnessy; Piper Jaffray Companies, Inc.; Ritz Foundation; John and Beverly Rollwagen
Fund of the Minneapolis Foundation; The St. Paul Companies, Inc.; Star Tribune/Cowles
Media Foundation; James R. Thorpe Foundation; Lila Wallace-Reader's Digest Literary
Publishers Marketing Development Program, funded through a grant to the
Council of Literary Magazines and Presses; and generous individuals.

Library of Congress Cataloging-in-Publication Data

Rogers, Pattiann, 1940–
    Eating bread and honey / Pattiann Rogers. — 1st ed.
      p. cm.
    ISBN 1-57131-406-7
    I. Title
PS3568.0454E38   1997
811'.54—dc21   96-46697
                                                                          CIP

This book is printed on acid-free paper.

For my sons and my daughter,
Arthur, John, and Lisa

My gratitude and love to very good friends who have given me support, enriching conversations, and companionship during the time when the poems in this book were being written. Very special thanks to my agent, Elizabeth Grossman, and to my editor, Emilie Buchwald, for her insight and many helpful suggestions.

Eating Bread and Honey

Eating Bread and Honey

BOOK ONE

The Singing Place

For the orange, saucer-eyed
lemurs indri of the family sifaka,
it is the perfect forest of the hot,
humid zones. There, at sunset and dawn,
they all pause arboreally and chorus,
howling, hooting, shaking the shadows
overhead, the fruits and burrowing
beetles inside the many-storied
jungle. They are the ushers,
the chaperones, the screaming
broadcast of darkness and light.

The house cricket, the field cricket,
the dead-leaf cricket make song places
of the warmest, darkest niches
they can find, at the bases of stones,
in grass stem funnels, the mossy
underbark of southside tree trunks.

For the sage grouse, male, the real
singing place is where he actually sings,
there inside the thimble-sized, flesh-
and-blood place of his voice, that air
sac burbling and popping, puffing
through the morning as he struts
and bows before his hens on the open
spring lek. Breath, I believe,
is place.

And maybe even the bulb and tuber
and root suck of the big black slug
of wet pastures could be called a long,

slow mud music and meter of sustenance,
by those lucky enough to be born
with a pasture sense for sound.

The whine and wind of heat
through ragged gorges make sandstone
and basalt a moving song. And place,
I think, is moments in motion.

As on the white-statue plains
of the moon's most weird winter
where no dusk scream or lingering suck
or floosing air sac of song has ever
existed, utter stillness is a singing
place too, moments where I first
must find a shape of silence,
where I then must begin
to hum its structure.

Opus from Space

Almost everything I know is glad
to be born—not only the desert orangetip,
on the twist flower or tansy, shaking
birth moisture from its wings, but also the naked
warbler nestling, head wavering toward sky,
and the honey possum, the pygmy possum,
blind, hairless thimbles of forward,
press and part.

Almost everything I've seen pushes
toward the place of that state as if there were
no knowing any other—the violent crack
and seed-propelling shot of the witch hazel pod,
the philosophy implicit in the inside out
seed-thrust of the wood sorrel. All hairy
saltcedar seeds are single-minded
in their grasping of wind and spinning
for luck toward birth by water.

And I'm fairly shocked to consider
all the bludgeonings and batterings going on
continually, the head-rammings, wing-furors,
and beak-crackings fighting for release
inside gelatinous shells, leather shells,
calcium shells or rough, horny shells. Legs
and shoulders, knees and elbows flail likewise
against their womb walls everywhere, in pine
forest niches, seepage banks and boggy
prairies, among savannah grasses, on woven
mats and perfumed linen sheets.

Mad zealots, every one, even before
beginning they are dark dust-congealings

of pure frenzy to come into light.

Almost everything I know rages to be born,
the obsession founding itself explicitly
in the coming bone harps and ladders,
the heart-thrusts, vessels and voices
of all those speeding with clear and total
fury toward this singular honor.

The Fallacy of Thinking Flesh Is Flesh

Some part of every living creature
is always trembling, a curious
constancy in the wavering rims
of the cup coral, the tasseling
of fringe fish, in the polyrippling
of the polyclad flatworm even under the black
bottom water at midnight when nothing
in particular notices.

The single topknot, head feather,
of the horned screamer or the tufted
quail can never, in all its tethered
barbs and furs, be totally still.
And notice the plural flickers
of the puss moth's powdery antennae.
Not even the puss moth knows how
to stop them.

Maybe it's the pattern of the shattering
sea-moon so inherent to each body
that makes each more than merely body.
Maybe it's the way the blood possesses
the pitch and fall of blooming grasses
in a wind that makes the prairie
of the heart greater than its boundaries.
Maybe it's god's breath swelling
in the breast and limbs, like a sky
at dawn, that gives bright bone
the holiness of a rising sun.
There's more to flesh than flesh.

The steady flex and draw of the digger
wasp's blue-bulbed abdomen—I know

there's a fact beyond presence
in all that fidgeting.

Even as it sleeps, watch the body
perplex its definition—the slight shift
of the spine, the inevitable lash shiver,
signal pulse knocking. See, there,
that simple shimmer of the smallest
toe again, just to prove it.

Where Do Your People Come From?

Great-grandfather originated
inside the seamless shell of a hickory nut,
being enabled, thereby, to see
in blindness the future brightness
of combusting seeds and the sun's dark
meat captured in walls like night.

Three aunts came up through the roots
of raspberries, rhododendrons and oaks
and so perceive prophecy in the water-seeking
lines of the moon, in the urging branches
of the incantatory voice. They perceive
the sweet fruits and blossoms thriving
unwitnessed in the plane above the stars.

My sisters were spun outward
from the pinion and swirling-lariat swim
of seals under ice. They walk on earth,
therefore, with bodies as smooth
and radiant as daylight through snow.
Each opens to her lover with the same
giving grace hidden in the fur-warmth
of a seal inclining toward surges,
turning passion round, round in currents
slowly, then heading fast for heaven.

From the line between rock and sky
come my brothers who hold measure
and lock in one hand, hold flocking
violet-green swallows and thin, shining
robes of rain in the emptiness
of the other hand, brothers who swell

with the blue space of mercy
in their stone-steady bones.

My cousins rose right out of the *cheery,*
cheery, cheery chu cry of the painted redstart.
Thus they think in terms of three two-turning
leaves and one hanging plum, seven-syllable
gods, three open windows and a single latched
door, six stitches of scarlet silk—three
in, three out—and a final knot.

And I, rising up through sedimentary
earth—fossil femur, jaw and shell,
burrow and track—speak as I must,
in just this way, of all beginning
points of origin.

Orange Thicket:
To Speak in Tongues

A god lives inside the orange,
a divinity partitioned who discusses
the eight sections of his own being
one at a time with his seven other voices,
an important lesson for the versification
of all future scriptures.

And the orange tells time. It ticks,
sliding in sequential explosions
from its green pea-skull emergence
out of white petals into the measured
dissolves of its wrinkling mold
and powder collapse into a nothing
and new beginning zero.

Some ancient oranges are at the bottom
of the sea, having fallen that far
off the railings of ships sailing
the Indian Ocean or having been dragged
down inside the cargo bays of sinking
ships Italy-bound. There, in the fright
of that deaf and smother of black
salt and tonnage, they testify still
to the existence of sky noise and sun.

The Maltese, red-pulped, doesn't speak
in sound but postulates to summer, evidences
to the round scarlets and brass vowels
of dawn, the burnished sermons of dusk.

Orange-girls with their carts filled, orange-
wenches rolling their loaded wheelbarrows,

vendors of orange-wood walking sticks—all
shout orange praises through the streets
every day in their wondrous rags.

In Parfait Amour, the orange as bitters
speaks with limes, rose spirits
and spices, to all lovers who will taste.

With a tangible voice, a sweet speech
of rind oils and juices, with a cry
of passion that possesses weight
in the hands and baskets of Moors
and Chinese queens, the orange
wants, above all in its spiritual
sizzle, never to die.

Murder in the Good Land

       Murder among the creek narrows
and shafts of rice grass, among lacy
coverlets and field sacks, among basement
apple barrels and cellar staples
of onion and beet;
                     beneath piled stones,
razed, broken and scattered stones,
beneath cow bridges, draw bridges, T girders
crossed, and cables, beneath brome, spadefoot,
beneath roots of three-awn
                     and heaven; murder
in the sky between stalks of spikesedge,
between harrier and wolf willow, between
the bedroom walls of formidable sluts
and saints, in the sad blindnesses
of moon and mole, in light as curt
and clearcut as blades of frost
magnified;
              through blanks of winter wind
through summer soapweed, through welcoming
gates and bolted gates, throughout the blood-rushing
grief of the swarmy sea;
                  murder beside gods
down heathen colonnades, down corridors of scholars
and beggars, down the cathedral colonnades
of orchards in harvest;
                    murder with the clench
of white clover, with the slip of the wandering
tattler, with the slow splash of window
curtains flowing inward
               with morning air; murder
in the winsome, murder in the wayward,

murder in canyon wrens, in the low beating bell
in the womb, in bone rafters,

                                 in mushroom
rings and rosy rings; murder, murder,
murder immortal, pervasive, supreme
everywhere in the good land.

Nearing Autobiography

Those are my bones rifted
and curled, knees to chin,
among the rocks on the beach,
my hands splayed beneath my skull
in the mud. Those are my rib
bones resting like white sticks
wracked on the bank, laid down,
delivered, rubbed clean
by river and snow.

Ethereal as seedless weeds
in dim sun and frost, I see
my own bones translucent as locust
husks, light as spider bones,
as filled with light as lantern
bones when the candle flames.
And I see my bones, facile,
willing, rolling and clacking,
reveling like broken shells
among themselves in a tumbling surf.

I recognize them, no other's,
raggedly patterned and wrought,
peeled as a skeleton of sycamore
against gray skies, stiff as a fallen
spruce. I watch them floating
at night, identical lake slivers
flush against the same star bones
drifting in scattered pieces above.

Everything I assemble, all
the constructions I have rendered
are the metal and dust of my locked
and storied bones. My bald cranium
shines blind as the moon.

Of Possibility:
Another Autumn Leaving

Here they come like miniature herds
of headless ponies without hooves,
stampeding, rearing, trampling one another.
They corral to circle upward themselves
like airborne droves of crippled brown
crows, rising in fragments of dust spouts,
raining down singly in swiveling pieces.

As if they were blind, they batter
against barricades, pile along brick
walls, boulders, wooden fences, filling
gullies and clefts, multitudes deep
as if they had no need to breathe.
Even with bodies without lungs,
there's a ghost cusp and sigh, a hollow
desert buzz to their rousing.

They sweep all night in the dry-moon
rasp of their rattling trance.
They scutter and reel up the windowpanes
on their hundred pins, over the roof
in their thorny flocks. Though totally
lacking bones or the tatters of bones,
still they shrivel and quake.
Though totally devoid of hearts
or the rubbish of hearts, still
they are brittle and heedless.

Even without souls, they shiver and rend.
Even without devils, they make ritual

processions of their deprivations. With no
word at all, they lie. They stutter.
They testify to themselves. Even lost
and without a god, they make visions
of the invisible, become the buffet,
the possessed, the very place of wind.
They are the time and tangible nexus
of all heavenly spirits. Even without tongues,
they clatter their tongues.

Creation by the Presence of Absence:
City Coyote in Rain

She's sleek blue neon through
the blue of the evening. She's black
sheen off the blue of wet streets,
blue daunt of suspension in each
pendant of rain filling the poplars
on the esplanade.

Her blue flank flashes once in the panes
of empty windows as she passes.
She's faster than lighthouse blue
sweeping the seas in circles.

Like the leaping blue of flames
burning in an alley barrel, her presence
isn't perceived until she's gone.

She cries with fat blue yelps, calls
with the scaling calls of the ragmen,
screeches a siren of howls along the docks
below the bridges, wails with the punctuated
griefs of drunks and orphans.

She scuttles under gates, through doors
hanging by broken hinges, behind ash
bins, into a culvert, shakes off the storm
in an explosion of radiance, licks
the cold muzzles and genitals of her frenzied
pups, gives them her blue teats, closes
her yellow eyes.

No one ever sees her face to face,
or those who do never know they do,

denying her first, pre-empting her lest
the place of pattern and time she creates,
like the blue of a star long since
disintegrated, enter their hearts
with all of its implications.

The Death of Living Rocks
and the Consequences Thereof

The god of rocks said *stop,*
and all the rocks stopped still
where they were—wolf rocks, pouncing
or suckling, packed in the forest,
snake rocks singling over the desert,
rock toads, their round pebbly
humps huddled along streambeds.

They all stopped—whale boulders
impassive on the floor of the sea, seal
rocks piled shiny and herded in spray
on the shore, a rock puma, granite
teeth bared, her rock kittens scattered
and halted halfway down the hill,
closed mica butterfly wings

Whole swaths of gypsum stobs
and flowerets became paralyzed
where we see them now, unmoved
in the wind. Pipes of organ rocks
and the red bugle rocks beside them
posed statuesque over ravines
and gulches without music.

On the day the god of rocks
said *stop,* all the rocks of the earth
stood still, without further expression,
without further response. And the god
of rocks, simply a possible reflection
of his own rock creation, became bound himself,
eyes staring marble white, voice a solid
layer of shale, the words *live again*
soundless and locked irretrievably
on his silent, stone tongue.

The Consequences of Death

You might previously have thought
each death just a single loss.
But when a plain gray titmouse dies,
what plunges simultaneously and disappears too
are all the oak-juniper woodlands,
the streamside cottonwoods, every elderberry
bush and high spring growth of sprouted
oak once held inside its eye.

And when a sugar pine splits, breaks
to the ground, falling with its fiestas
and commemorations of blue-green needles,
long-winged seeds, the sweet resin
of its heartwood, there's another
collapse coincident—a fast inward
sinking and sucking back to nothing
of all those stars once kept in its core,
those clusters of suns and shining
dusts once resident in the sky of its rigid
bark and cone-scales. We could hear
the sound of that galactic collapse as well,
if we had the proper ears for it.

And when a mountain sheep stumbles,
plummets, catapulting skull, spine,
from cliff side to crumbling rock below,
a like shape of flame and intensity
on a similar sharp ledge on the other side
of the same moment, out of our sense,
loses balance, goes blind.

Because of these torn paper-shreds
of gold-lashed wings, this spangled

fritillary's death, somewhere behind the night
a convinced declaration of air and matter
and intention, silenced, speaks no longer
of the god of its structure.

Against the Ethereal

I'm certain these are the only angels
there are: those with raised, sneering
lips revealing razor-pure incisors that rip
with a purpose, dominions in the moment
when they spread like flying squirrels,
sail like jaguarundi across the celestials
with sickle claws thrust forward.

This is the only rite of holiness
I know: fierce barb of bacteria, that hot,
hot coal, that smoldering challenge
glaring, for twelve millennia at least,
in all directions from its dark, subzero
cellar of frozen, glacial rock.

This is the noise of heavenly
hosts: trumpet-blaring chaparrals
and shinneries, cymbal-banging greasewood
and jojoba deserts, burble of hellbinders, slips
of heliotropes, tweakings of brush mice
and big-eared bats, wheezings of rusty wheels,
grasshopper sparrows, autumn leaves ticking
across gravel on their paper pricks.

I aspire devotedly and with all reverence
to the raspy links of lampreys, the tight
latchings of pawpaw apples and soursops,
the perfect piercings and fastenings
of sperms and ovipositors, clinging
grasps of titis and chacmas.

Aren't you peculiarly frightened, as I am,
by the vague, the lax, the gossamer

and faint, the insubstantial and all
submissive, bowing transparencies,
any willfully pale worshipping?

This is the only stinging, magenta-cruel,
fire-green huffing, bellowing mayhemic
spirituality I will ever recognize:
the one shuddering with veined lightning,
chackling with seeded consolations, howling
with winter pities, posturing with speared
and fisted indignations, surly as rock, rude
as weeds, riotous as billbugs, tumultuous
as grapevine beetles, as large black, burying
beetles, bare, uncovered to every perception
of god, and never, never once forgiving
death.

Service with Benediction

Chunk honey, creamed honey, buckwheat
honey on buckwheat bread—like glass lanterns,
there's enough concentrated summer sun caught
in these jars of comb honey to give us
ample light to travel by on a winter night.

Sesame breads, sausage breads, almond
breads, sweet panettones, cassava cakes
and millet cakes, all are laid out
on the table before me beside these bowls
of molasses honey and heather honey, wild-
wood honey gathered by wild bees, hallows
of honey, orisons of bulging loaves.

So I eat sun and earth by the slice
and spoonful, suck yeast breads soaked
in alfalfa honey, dip crusts dripping
from the dish to my mouth, lick gold
sugar from my fingers. I swallow
pure flower syrup brought from the sky,
chew the kneaded spike and germ of fields
and gardens. Surely I become then
all the arabesques of bee dances
and the cultures of beebread balls rolled
from nectar pollen. I comply easily
with the lean of heady buds and grasses
waxing and waning at their cores
sunk in the earth.

Two gifts, I heard the temple bakers say,
when, for immortality, the priests immersed

his dead body naked before burial
in a cistern of amber honey.

Allow me now in the fullness of this morning
to consume enough clover honey and white
wheat fire to see my way clearly
through the cold night coming.

BOOK TWO

Animals and People:
"The Human Heart in Conflict with Itself"

Some of us like to photograph them. Some
of us like to paint pictures of them. Some of us
like to sculpt them and make statues and carvings
of them. Some of us like to compose music
about them and sing about them. And some of us
like to write about them.

Some of us like to go out
and catch them and kill them and eat them. Some
of us like to hunt them and shoot them and eat them.
Some of us like to raise them, care for them and eat
them. Some of us just like to eat them.

And some of us
name them and name their seasons and name their hours,
and some of us, in our curiosity, open them up
and study them with our tools and name their parts.
We capture them, mark them and release them,
and then we track them and spy on them and enter
their lives and affect their lives and abandon
their lives. We breed them and manipulate them
and alter them. Some of us experiment
upon them.

We put them on tethers and leashes,
in shackles and harnesses, in cages and boxes,
inside fences and walls. We put them in yokes
and muzzles. We want them to carry us and pull us
and haul for us.

And we want some of them
to be our companions, some of them to ride on our fingers
and some to ride sitting on our wrists or on our shoulders

and some to ride in our arms, ride clutching our necks.
We want them to walk at our heels.

We want them to trust
us and come to us, take our offerings, eat from our hands.
We want to participate in their beauty. We want to assume
their beauty and so possess them. We want to be kind
to them and so possess them with our kindness and so
partake of their beauty in that way.

And we want them
to learn our language. We try to teach them our language.
We speak to them. We put *our* words in *their* mouths.
We want *them* to speak. We want to know what they see
when they look at us.

We use their heads and their bladders
for balls, their guts and their hides and their bones
to make music. We skin them and wear them for coats,
their scalps for hats. We rob them, their milk
and their honey, their feathers and their eggs.
We make money from them.

We construct icons of them.
We make images of them and put their images on our clothes
and on our necklaces and rings and on our walls
and in our religious places. We preserve their dead
bodies and parts of their dead bodies and display
them in our homes and buildings.

We name mountains
and rivers and cities and streets and organizations
and gangs and causes after them. We name years and time
and constellations of stars after them. We make mascots

of them, naming our athletic teams after them. Sometimes
we name ourselves after them.

We make toys of them
and rhymes of them for our children. We mold them
and shape them and distort them to fit our myths
and our stories and our dramas. We like to dress up
like them and masquerade as them. We like to imitate them
and try to move as they move and make the sounds they make,
hoping, by these means, to enter and become the black
mysteries of their being.

Sometimes we dress them
in our clothes and teach them tricks and laugh at them
and marvel at them. And we make parades of them
and festivals of them. We want them to entertain us
and amaze us and frighten us and reassure us
and calm us and rescue us from boredom.

We pit them
against one another and watch them fight one another,
and we gamble on them. We want to compete with them
ourselves, challenging them, testing our wits and talents
against their wits and talents, in forests and on plains,
in the ring. We want to be able to run like them and leap
like them and swim like them and fly like them and fight
like them and endure like them.

We want their total
absorption in the moment. We want their unwavering devotion
to life. We want their oblivion.

Some of us give thanks
and bless those we kill and eat, and ask for pardon,

and this is beautiful as long as they are the ones dying
and we are the ones eating.

And as long as we are not
seriously threatened, as long as we and our children
aren't hungry and aren't cold, we say, with a certain
degree of superiority, that we are no better
than any of them, that any of them deserve to live
just as much as we do.

And after we have proclaimed
this thought, and by so doing subtly pointed out
that we are allowing them to live, we direct them
and manage them and herd them and train them and follow
them and map them and collect them and make specimens
of them and butcher them and move them here and move
them there and we place them on lists and we take
them off of lists and we stare at them and stare
at them and stare at them.

We track them in our sleep.
They become the form of our sleep. We dream of them.
We seek them with accusation. We seek them
with supplication.

And in the ultimate imposition,
as Thoreau said, we make them bear the burden
of our thoughts. We make them carry the burden
of our metaphors and the burden of our desires and our guilt
and carry the equal burden of our curiosity and concern.
We make them bear our sins and our prayers and our hopes

into the desert, into the sky, into the stars.
We say we kill them for God.

　　　　　　　　We adore them and we curse
them. We caress them and we ravish them. We want them
to acknowledge us and be with us. We want them to disappear
and be autonomous. We abhor their viciousness and lack
of pity, as we abhor our own viciousness and lack of pity.
We love them and we reproach them, just as we love
and reproach ourselves.

　　　　　　　　We will never, we cannot,
leave them alone, even the tiniest one, ever, because we know
we are one with them. Their blood is our blood. Their breath
is our breath, their beginning our beginning, their fate
our fate.

　　　　　　Thus we deny them. Thus we yearn
for them. They are among us and within us and of us,
inextricably woven with the form and manner of our being,
with our understanding and our imaginations.
They are the grit and the salt and the lullaby
of our language.

　　　　　　　　We have a need to believe they are there,
and always will be, whether we witness them or not.
We need to know they are there, a vigorous life maintaining
itself without our presence, without our assistance,
without our attention. We need to know, we *must* know,

that we come from such stock so continuously and tenaciously
and religiously devoted to life.

We know we are one with them,
and we are frantic to understand how to actualize that union.
We attempt to actualize that union in our many stumbling,
ignorant and destructive ways, in our many confused
and noble and praiseworthy ways.

For how can we possess dignity
if we allow them no dignity? Who will recognize our beauty
if we do not revel in their beauty? How can we hope
to receive honor if we give no honor? How can we believe
in grace if we cannot bestow grace?

We want what we cannot
have. We want to give life at the same moment
we are taking it, nurture life at the same moment we light
the fire and raise the knife. We want to live, to provide,
and not be instruments of destruction, instruments
of death. We want to reconcile our "egoistic concerns"
with our "universal compassion." We want the lion
and the lamb to be one, the lion and the lamb
within finally to dwell together, to lie down together
in peace and praise at last.

BOOK THREE

The Art of Raising Gibbons and Flowers

We think they go well together—the translucent
vanilla orchid, the slipper orchid, the ginger
fragrances of the fiddle leaf, the swollen,
juice-filled buds of magnolia grandiflora,
Turkish tulip, Susa crocus, and the Siamang
gibbons who pound and scream, quarreling
and sweating, stinking inside their tight
cages where we have put them in the garden
under the iron oak trees.

They shake the bars, their snouts
dripping, piles of fecal matter covered
with green flies in the corners of their cages.
How they reek, puffing their red throat sacs
to holler and hoot in chorus at dawn and dusk.
The petals of the fringed iris and the tea-scented
China rose certainly shimmer then with that roar,
and even pollen spores and feeding butterflies
are shaken loose by the fetid blast.

But it all makes a nice contrast, we think.
So we let the ranging wisteria venture over
the east brick wall without pruning, the grape
hyacinths spill supremely beyond the borders
of the walk. The spirea and trumpet vines
billow up through summer at will
like surf in a storm.

And the wide, white cups of gloriosa
blossoms hang down soft, confident
and abundant from the branches of the iron oak
where their vines have climbed. In an evening

breeze, we see them brush the roofs of those rank
cages, dawdle there in an evening breeze.
They sway and hush out of sight. Their perfume
and nectar-rain are dizzying. Their petals
shine with moonlight, just barely beyond
the reach of the horny black fingers stretching
through the bars to scratch, to encase.

Later we come close to the cages to watch
the gibbons sleeping, the straggly hairy
nakedness of their curled bodies. We imagine
they dream that the crusty callouses and bunions
of their hands and feet have turned to camellias,
to petals of pale nolana, that they sip the liquor
of honeysuckle and drink the ices of violets
and orange blossoms. We imagine they dream
that their arms and torsos are supple
vines and sturdy trunks rising unrestrained
into the night, carrying moonlight
on the blossoms and graces of their bodies
up through the sky and back to the source
of that shining.

There's a certain pity and hope
made evident by this, which is the art
we carry with us like a penance out of the garden,
along the path, and down the darkened
hallways to our beds.

Partners

1.

I like sleeping with the old table leg
close beside me under the covers in bed.
It's so placid, still and sturdy
in its slumber. It tolerates my knee
hooked over its finely lathed middle
and the way our ankles and feet
couple beneath the blanket.

Without attention or liberty (unlike
window or mirror), it withdraws wholly
and satisfactorily into the tight
oak of its own parameters.

Hardly restless, it never resists
itself or cants recitations to maker
or scholars. Its respiration is a lasting
lullaby, more predictable than my breath,
its heart less phantom, more upholding
than my heart.

During winter snows, I seek it,
I cradle it to my bed, I tuck it.
We somnia close, belly to belly
all through the night of the night.

2.

I like sleeping with great-uncle's
sea-crusted rope. I wind it in the familiar
route up my legs, round my waist, between
my breasts, a repeated necklace.

My sleep composes to its spirals,
follows its blind underwater passages,

the lines of its many past knots
loosened and lost.

The light of its fragrant coils
is the silver of its lovely residue:
dried spittle, fish flakes, moon oil.

With its head-end like a thumb
stuck in my mouth in the dark, subsumed,
I suck the salt-jack of its prehistoric
waves and currents.

3.

I take the carefully tuned guitar along
to sleep with me at night. Wrought
below the frets with ivory crescent moons
and their ebony crescent shadows,
it reclines best on its back, keeping
to its own pillow, keys resting
against the fringed satin.

With a mere accidental brush of my hand
across the center of its nakedness
in the dark, I feel the two of us
and the entire bed, springs and boards alike,
become a humming, six-stringed doxology.

The guitar surrounds a hollowness
as desperate as my sleep inside
its framework, as immeasurable as the night
inside its boundaries, as possible
as any truth inside its fabrication,
and sings the same.

Kissing a Kit Fox

The kit fox has fine lips. Often black
or gray, they are as demure as two slight
fronds of Mayweed in fog, yet a little fuller.
They are capable of pulling back,
disappearing up and into the nether
to reveal his impressive fangs.

The lips of the kit fox taste
sometimes of the sweet spring water
he drank in its dark rock the moment before.
They taste also sometimes of the rank
bone marrow of the dead peccary
he licked in the ditch for a meal.
His lips and breath today tasted
of the peanut of desiccated
grasshoppers burned dry.

The needle teeth of the kit fox
when kissing sometimes pierce the lover's
tongue with sevenfold hot spears
like the sun. Often too they puncture
the lips of the lover and bring blood
to the mouth like the moon. A few cherish
this pain when kissing the kit fox,
because they believe they then may speak
with the authority of scars
on the nature of day and night.

And when kissing a kit fox,
some are lucky, for he will occasionally
wrap the thick ragrances of his plush
tail around the lover's neck up to the ears,

or better, across the eyes and over the nose.
One may then fall completely into the lush
swoon and smother of his race and art—cactus
juice, thorns and the musk of fear, snake
seed, fecal rat.

Some say kissing the kit fox
is a story, because it has both character
and event, both union and scorn.
But some say it is a song in syncopation
that they may tap to themselves
in loneliness for comfort. Others say kissing
the kit fox is a place one may enter,
a location with boundaries fixed in space,
a measurable site in a portion of time.
I say kissing a kit fox is like memory,
because it is a mere invention of pleasure
and pain, a creation of wild risk
with wound and fetish, certain evidence
of either the unlikely or the lost.

Kaleidoscope:
Free Will and the Nature of the Holy Spirit

At the beginning, the Lady of Wild
Things is placed cheek-to-cheek
with her long-fingered, woolly black
lemur aye-aye, while Baby Bob, decked
and dingled in silver fleece, sleeps
where he was laid—in his cradle
under a creamy summer moon. The nootka
rose can only spread and spin itself
like a philosophy all night
over the crooked garden walk.

Suddenly, a playful twist of the instrument,
and there's the Lady upside down
at the top now, her purple silk tights
tight up her legs certainly kicking
in the sky. The full wondrous tail
of the aye-aye is curled seductively
around the fat cheeks of the tilting
summer moon during this moment, and Baby
Bob, spilled from his cradle, finds
himself wound close, locked in the prose
of nootka roses.

The inevitable rotation again,
and Baby Bob is sucking sweet cream
from the fallen moon nestled-in now
beside him. The lemur aye-aye, landing
sprawled in a seduction of nootka roses,
tickles with one long finger the purple
dingles at the center of each cheeky
blossom. Spinning crookedly, the Lady

can't help chasing the wondrous tail
of the wild black night circling fast
and free in her eyes.

All are tumbled once more, and a new
crescent moon is set to swaying as a result,
rocking like an empty cradle of light
suspended mid-garden. The Lady of Wild
Things Tamed kisses, as she must, the sweet
creamy cheeks of Baby Bob pressed against
her perfect nootka rose mouth. Decked
in silver fleece pajamas and flipped
topsy-turvy, the aye-aye walks
on its hands across the summer night
like a shiny moon with black feet
thrust upward among the dingling stars.

The whole world is shaken again,
and this time the shiny round rock
of the moon is stuck firmly in the aye-aye's
mouth, whereby its eyes are lit brightly
to shine like summer. The night has become
a cradle of philosophy rocking a sleeping
nootka rose to stone (perfect definition
of a pink moon blooming) which the Lady
is compelled to pluck and wear
in her ear for cheer to Baby Bob.

O Lady, take the full moon like a monocular
glass, hold it to your eye, if you can,

and study. O aye-aye, with your crooked
finger beckon the rosy summer night,
gently tickle Baby Bob's cream-dabbled
chin, play dingle long and loudly
on the truth of these turnings.

Inside the Universe Inside the Act

The plum, just picked, is smooth
and cold as a river stone in the hand,
egg-smooth along the lips, soft
as lips against the lips. Its quick
puncture at the teeth is discrete,
the tongue of its brown-syrup-
fragrance. Inside this event
of bone and tree, this consumation
of plum weather and sugar pulp
swallowed, is a singular universe
created alone of ripe purple,
pit, savor and summer signature.

The staggered moonlight off cracked
and shackled grasses of ice, the white
piece of moonlight the baby wants
to lift from his blanket, the smoke
of moonlight in the panting breath
of the cougar caught in a trap—
these are not the same moonlight.
Even in the same instant of winter
evening, each is a multiple, rare
universe itself determining the universe.

What unique writing is plucked
by the rain's passage across the lake
this evening? What line of the world
is only recorded by water falling
at dusk on water? How should
the histories of electrons read now
inside these dissolving signals
of storm? And what reality at last

is created, set spinning like a globe
in orbit, by the act of asking questions
of the rain within the rain?

Night and the swift prescriptions
of stars rise, collapse, join,
and dissemble, change relevancy again
and again inside this hour—my hands
in love, in light along your face,
your hands beneath my thighs, my legs
parted for you, hidden, vulnerable
underbelly exposed for you.

Every leaf of every plum in moonlight,
all rain prophecies, all dissolutions
of all swallowed suns are shaken
forever inside the rile of our bound
bodies, inside our cries
of compassion for far-flying
distances and their poor solitudes.

Now inside this first remembering—what new
place becomes? what time begins?

The Center of the Known Universe

It's exactly here—mark the moment—the tip
of my breast kissed and held
in his mouth, now the one clear grain
around which all goldfish gather to nip
and feed and fleck their fire, now
the circling ring where all river
waters descend, swelling and surging,
this tight bud in his mouth
whose petals, thin as light, I feel
as they loose themselves singly,
peel away like breath, falling
by falling, dissolve only to rise again.
By this falling I understand
how resurrection is central
to knowing.

And this moment is congruent,
the very same moment where Mother
often held Father cradled to her breast,
the same exact moment where Mary nursed
the Christ child feeding, that bud,
that mouth pulling. Astral bodies,
we remember, were drawn into orbit
around that place. By this I understand
how event gives order to matter.

Found nipple nestled in the warmth
of his nudging mouth, inside the curled
and sucking funnel of his tongue—
this is the central bead of the only
universe I know, the very pin
around which the open window, the white

sheet pushed to my knees, the house,
its dishes and doors and eaves,
the curlew calling in the fields outside,
all go whirling. It is the hub where I
in my own knowing go swinging round,
eyes closed, head above, head below.
My toes, my fingertips define
themselves properly only by measuring
their circumferences circling this axis.

God bless the small, central power
and point of this loving instant
upon which all angels, forever countless,
bore and spin and pivot, naked angels
embracing naked angels, mouths at breasts
everywhere inside the center of this moment
holding time and its great wheeling
lariat fixed and found and knowable.

Place and Proximity

I'm surrounded by stars. They cover me
completely like an invisible silk veil
full of sequins. They touch me, one by one,
everywhere—hands, shoulders, lips,
ankle hollows, thigh reclusions.

Particular in their presence, like rain,
they come also in streams, in storms.
Careening, they define more precisely
than wind. They enter, cheekbone,
breastbone, spine, skull, moving out
and in and out, through like threads,
like weightless grains of beads
in their orbits and rotations,
their ritual passages.

They are the luminescence of blood
and circuit the body. They are showers
of fire filling the dark, myriad spaces
of porous bone. What can be nearer
to flesh than light?

And I swallow stars. I eat stars.
I breathe stars. I survive on stars.
They sound precisely, humming in my nose,
in my throat, on my tongue. *Stars, stars.*

They are above me suspended, drifting,
caught in the loom of the elm, similarly enmeshed
in my hair. They are below me straight down

in the deep. I am immersed in stars. I swim
through stars, their swells and currents.
I walk on stars. They are less,
they are more, even than water,
even than earth.

They come with immediacy. They are as bound
to me as history. No knife, no death
can part us.

The Kingdom of Heaven

      inside of which careen
the wrecked suns of obliterating
stellar furies and smelting quasars
ejecting the seething matter of stars
in piercing shocks wrenching and spewing
blasted flares and ash of incinerated
planets whose roaring eruptions
and scorching thunders, in the slightest
proximity, would boil and melt the ear
to spent char long before those sounds
could ever reach the ear as sound
      inside of which exist
the serenities of this fading summer
evening, the motion of wind in slow,
shifting passions down from redcedar
and netleaf, across the easy flight
of creeks and bluegrasses, within
the peace of possibilities created
by a single cricket in his place,
the assurance of blindnesses behind
my eyes closed on this hillside,
earth pressing against my body
      inside of which wheel
fine solar particles and microscopic
constellations issuing and collapsing,
waging transformations, gatherings
and dissolutions through bones and veins,
circling and spinning in pursuits and purposes
with bloody powers and strategies
      inside of which is one
deity proven by the faith of sleep
and the imagination to exist throughout
these realms of such measured light
and destruction

Fractal:
Repetition of Form over a Variety of Scales

This moment is a single blue jay,
a scramble of flint, sapphire iron,
spiking blue among the empty brambles
and vines wound like skeins back
upon themselves through the dun forest
of thistle spurs and thorns.

And this moment is as well the brambled
skeleton of the jay, anthracite spine,
thorny blades and femurs, tangle
of knuckled twigs flittering
through an equal flitter of jointed
sticks, vines and husks of wind.

And as well again, this split second
is the singular blue-black pod of jay heart
thiddering among a bramble of rib bones
inside the tufts, the bristled
capsules of forest and winter barbed
and strung with dusk.

And the jay's call is this same
instant, a cry of release slivered
and shaped by the tangle of bones
and scrub woods, by the bolus wound
of winter air, thatched and spurred,
through which it travels.

And this moment is a single point
of sun wrapped and templing in the black
pathways of the blue jay's eye, like a heart
shuddering in a tangle of bones,
like a bird in a shifting knot of forest,
a call in a skeletal patch of winter,

winter in a weaving clutch of dusk, a moment
tangling within the string and bristle
of its own vocabulary.

God is a process, a raveled nexus
forever tangling into and around the changing
form of his own moment—pulse and skein,
shifting mien, repeating cry
of loss and delivery.

Within One Moment, All Possible Moments

Across the plains, over the threadleaf
and the gripping thistle, Mignon comes running
up to the edge of the crevasse, stops short, peers
down into those shifting halls, the seeping
guano, the latched and bundled
fluttering pods of the netherness.

Running across the plains, her eyes
on the metal marker ahead, a pole
of the circumnavigating medicine line,
Mignon, not aware of the crevasse, falls
sideways into it, is transformed in that deep
harrow to a planted seed of Reseda ordorata,
mignonette rooted, little greenish-white flower.

Mignon, lithe and fleet, becomes
her running so thoroughly that she crosses
the crevasse in one stride, never seeing
nor knowing afterward in her hartebeest
bed, beneath her antelope covers,
within the gazelle of her sleep, anything
of the immobile gulf of its terror.

From a mile away, she sprints right for it,
dives deliberately headfirst straight down
into that crevasse, her long, full skirts
falling completely over her head,
revealing beneath, in place of legs, a jester
in a spotted overcoat who seizes a juniper
with his bejangled hands, holds tight,
blinking at the sudden light.

Mignon steps into that element slowly,
carefully, one foot off the dusty grass,

then the other, sinks, the blackness pulling
like a drawstring over her head. She floats
through scattered incendiary dust; occasionally
here and there, she hears a hist of tight flames
beading tighter. She drifts directly
for the spot where the moon used to be.

After leading her mother right
to god's mouth, shoving her over and down
into that chasm, Mignon closes the crevasse,
as if it were a book, turns off the light
beside the bed, pulls the blanket to her chin,
shuts her eyes, steps out in her running shoes
onto the quiet snow-covered plains.

Remembering the Present Tense

Before I was a ghost, I was born.
This event was continuous—as the separating
and peeling away of beetle and barnacle
shells, of birchleaf and curlleaf from the sun
is continuous, as the unraveling of sage,
saltcedar and thrasher from the day
is continuous.

I was born a ghost. There were no
boundaries between me and the fragrances
of wild grape and licorice. The light
of fireflea, fox eye, dropseed, candelabra
tree, all entered me freely. I gazed myself
without shape or name right into the hard
glass monocle of the moon, descended bodiless
through water into the fibrillating black
dollop of tadpole. I penetrated the boll
of the buckbrush, merged with the thump
of the bushtit. In one sudden opening
of layered clouds, I became all the moments
in a moment of summer night.

I was a ghost forever before I was born,
bearing in the presence of what was to come
the entirety of everything that had been—all past
holy distance and data of *now* held in the ovary
of the great-granddaughter of a son's unborn son.

When I was born into death,
I was a living ghost, being the only spirit
of fingers, the sole shock and rushing
spell of river litany, the animus of ponder

and strain. I was the abstraction
of my lips against his, the whimper
of longing, the revenant of hope. Reborn
and reborn, I was over and over the savage
soul of slaughter and consume.

I was born becoming the beginning
of a ghost dying. This finality was continuous—
the collapse of thunder into shingles
of rain merging into cactus canyons falling
into the gray claret of evening into the hollow
breath of the mud swallow disappearing
into the hall yard of night into curse
and its only other vanishing whole and powerful
together into their emergence.

The Immortal Soul

It longs for the spine-shudder
coming with an October persimmon
sucked clear to the seed. Legs,
thighs wound together in bed
mean everything to it.

It craves pipe and whistle
music played in neon reflections
on night rivers, seeks cello sounds
inside tangled sycamore shadows
at dusk. It falls in with the confusion
of waxwings and red ash disappearing
and emerging together in shifting
self-definitions of their own making.
The poverty of its isolation
is the royal totality of a crow
heard once at dawn calling
across the horizon.

Its first five ways are the first
five fragrances of bog and booth
willow, beaked sedge, blue clover,
blue grasses, encountered in the first
thaw of spring. The ten directions
of its faith are its two hands spread
before a blue-yellow flame burning
in the snow. The ways of its passion
are all the directions revealed by wet,
white needles in a pine forest
straining through riverfog.

It perceives the core of its name
as a wheel held by the hands, turned

full circle one way, then the other,
the range of its dominion as a wheel
spinning water, a rattling mill
wheeling wind, prophecy spinning
a fate, earth spinning the wheeling
properties of night.

Its most jolting connection to God
is headfirst off rocks down
into the pummeling pressure and sudden
suffocation of a cold surf.
Its most complete connection to God
are its naked feet cradled and kissed
by the most loved of lovers.
And when the voice of the one
lover is at its ear whispering
devotion and possession, telling
truthfully of such fictions, the soul
then believes with all of its body
in its own immortality.

Abundance and Satisfaction

1.

One butterfly is not enough. We need
many thousands of them, if only
for the effusion of the wayward-
swaying words they occasion—blue
and copper hairstreaks, sulphur
and cabbage whites, brimstones,
peacock fritillaries, tortoiseshell
emperors, skippers, meadow browns.
We need a multitude of butterflies
right on the tongue simply to be able
to speak with a varied six-pinned
poise and particularity.

But thousands of butterflies
are surfeit. We need just one
flitter to apprehend correctly
the will of aspen leaves, the lassitude
of lupine petals, the sleep
of a sleeping eyelid. To examine
adequately one set of finely leaded,
stained wings of violet translucence,
one single sucking proboscis (sap-
and-sugar-licking thread), to study
thoroughly just one powder scale, one
gold speck from one dusted butterfly
forewing would require at least
a millenium of attention to all melody,
phrase, gravity and horizon.

2.

And just the same, one moon is more
than sufficient, ample complexity

and bewilderment—single waning crescent,
waxing crescent, lone gibbous, one perfect,
solitary sickle and pearl, one map
of mountains and lava plains, Mare
Nectaris, Crater Tycho. And how could
anyone really hold more than one full
moon in one heart?

Yet one moon is not enough. We need
millions of moons, glossy porcelain
globes glowing as if from the inside out,
weaving among each other in the sky
like lanterns bobbing on a black river
sea-bound. Then we could study
moons and the traversings of moons
and the multiple meanings of the phases
of moons, and the eclipsing of moons
by one another. We need a new language
of moons containing all the syllables
of interacting rocks of light
so that we might fully understand,
at last, the phrase 'one heart
in many moons.'

3.
And of gods, we need just one, one
for the grief of twenty snow geese
frozen by their feet in ice and dead
above winter water. Yet we need twenty-
times-twenty gods for all the recurring

memories of twenty snow geese frozen
by their feet in sharp lake-water ice.

But a single god suffices
for the union of joys in one school
of invisible green-brown minnows
flocking over green-brown stones
in a clear spring, but three gods
are required to wind and unwind
the braided urging of spring—root,
blossom and spore. And we need
the one brother of gods for a fragged
plain, blizzard-split, battered
by tumbleweeds and wire fences,
and the one sister to mind
the million sparks and explosions
of gods on fire in a pine forest.

I want one god to be both scatter
and pillar, one to explain simultaneously
mercy and derision, yet a legion of gods
for the spools of confusion and design,
but one god alone to hold me by the waist,
to rumble and quake in my ear, to dance me
round and round, one couple with forty
gods in the heavenly background
with forty violins with one
immortal baton keeping time.

BOOK FOUR

"God Is in the Details,"
Says Mathematician Freeman J. Dyson

This is why grandmother takes such tiny
stitches, one stitch for each dust mote
of moon on the Serengeti at night, and one half
one stitch for each salt-fetch of fog
following the geometries of eelgrasses
in fields along the beach.

And this is why she changes the brief threads
in her glass needle so often—metallic bronze
for the halo around the thrasher's eye,
ruby diaphanous for the antenna tips
of the May beetle, transparent silk
for dry-rain fragrances blowing
through burr sages before rain.

She inserts her needle
through the center of each elementary
particle, as if it were a circling sequin
of blue, loops it to its orbit, sewing thus,
again and again, the reckless sapphire sea,
a whipping flag of tall summer sky.

Sometimes she takes in her hands
two slight breaths of needles at once,
needles so thin they almost burn
her fingers like splinters of light.
She crochets with them around each microscopic
void, invents, thereby, an ice tapestry
of winter on the window, creates a lace
of peeper shrillings through flooded
sweet gale, secures a blank jot of sight

in the knitting of each red flea
of zooplankton skittering mid-lake.

God's most minute exuberance is founded
in the way she sews with needles
as assertive as the sun-sharp loblolly
that she sees with her eyes closed;
in the way she knots stitches
as interlocked as the cries of veery,
peewee, black-capped chickadee and jay
that she hears with her ears stopped;
in the way she whispers to her work,
recites to her work, spooling every least
designation of spicule shade, hay
spider and air trifid, every hue
and rising act of her own hands. *Try
to escape now,* it reads, *just try.*

Mousefeet:
From a Lecture on Muridae Cosmology

Mousefeet are often as small, exact
and precocious as eighth notes penned
across a composer's score. Most are no
larger than two quarter-inch W's printed
side by side. All mouse toenails
are just about the size of poppy seeds.
Yet one encounters mousefeet
everywhere.

The leaves of the wild radish,
for instance, are simply green mousefeet
held bottomside up with thin toes spread
to the sun. And the leaves of aspens
and certain poplars make many mousefeet-
twitters-and-jumps themselves in any brief
skimpering mousebreath wind.

Each hister beetle, we know,
is just one fat, black mousefoot
transformed to bug.

Raindrops hitting dusty cement
sidewalks make trails of splayed mousefeet
running in every direction. And there are pale,
blue footprints of mice all over the moon.
Just get a telescope and check
for yourself some night.

Whitefooted mice in May create,
everywhere they step through the field,
those tiny white yarrow blossoms
so commonly seen. I've been exalted

as well by the musky whiffs of mousefeet
fragrances (moldy loam and leaf rot) rising
with wild cherry and green brier perfumes
through the damp night grasses,
haven't you?

Falling snowflakes caught on a dark wool
scarf are easily identified as the frozen,
crystal bones of pygmy mousefeet lost
in ice a century ago. You can feel
the prickle of cold scurry in your mouth
if you eat them.

And even after predators have speared
live mice and swallowed them whole, still,
those mousefeet are there, ticking
in the flick of the rattlesnake's tail,
scraping in the weasel's growl, running
and leaping with light in the cougar's
steady eye.

Be careful where you tread.
There are mousefeet, tiny folded fans
of knuckles and pins, thousands of them, curled
in the roll of the surf, inside the tight
furl of marsh fog, planted deep in pea pods,
and cockle rocks, in the earth in burrows
below us as we speak.

And be careful where you fly. They are startled,
a fleeing, overlapping four footprint dash

like dying dots of fire tracking
the black in multitudes across the night.

And be careful to listen
to exactly what your prayers are meaning
as you sing; for those mousefeet pervade
and determine, ping and sloop, dicker
and dodge through all invented cadences,
imposing on every voice and ear the tittering
character and mad, precise, alpha-and-omega
pickering machinery heard so prominently
every time in God's perfect reply.

Rapture of the Deep:
The Pattern of Poseidon's Love Song

The blue ornata's spiderweb
body sidles and pulses among the turning
cilia wheels of the microscopic
rotifera tilting over the feathery
fans of the splendidum slowly extending
and withdrawing
                              their fondling tongues
inside the body of the summer solstice
where the sun with its ragged
radiances organizes transparent
butterflies and paper kites of light
into flocks of meadow-drifting
throughout the green sea surrounding
the design
                    of string worms palolo
floating in the gripping and releasing
event of their own tight coils
toward a reef of chitons pulled
from their rock bases by the violent
bite and suck of a spinning
squall
              curling themselves then
into their round coat-of-mail shells
as if they were each one made
by the sound of long O moaning
inside a sailor's ancient prayer
to Mater Cara
                         tumbled and tumbled
by the waves beneath which the frilled
shark a singular presence in a dimension
of lesser constellations suspended
mid-sea whips with a graceful pattern

of pitiful evil
                    toward a nebula
of cephalopods undulating
below an arrangement of rain
shattering the evening suddenly
out of the linear into the million
falling moments
                    of one moment
pebbling the open plain of the sea
through which plankton ascend
like a legion of flittering spirits
or the single body of a multiple
deity swallowing stinging salt pieces
of stars
            to the surface to bask
beneath the violet order
of the traveling moon touching
all points in the declaration of birth
to death
            to stone embodied by shoals
of glass-threaded cod fluctuating
in their progress like schools of storm
petrels creating descent and angle
from a totally flat sky playing
a layering of flight
                    shadows off the eyes
of soaring dolphins breaching
with the contrapuntal rhythm of a passage
from Bach as over and within
this universe
                    the hand of an ecstatic
wind its fingers spread wide

with blessing moves in a seizure
of joy through every trembling spray
and pulse and skeleton forming
the reality of this whole
prolonged consummation

Going for Water and Light

Is it possible to draw up
in a bucket (that emptiness submerged
into the river and raised) both light
and its water? to pour water and light
together into the glass bowl
on the dinner table and not lose either?
by that crystal glass to cut light
into its needles of green-violet
and fire while keeping water
all the while whole?

Though moving water may remain
the one color of itself when seen properly,
yet light on rivers can be the copper-black
evening light of autumn or the blue-cinnamon
kerchief light of a morning in March,
the summer-lime underside light
of manna grasses swinging over the bank,
or the white belly-light of swallows
swooping above.

Lovers meet a little like water and light—
one coming down to the other, covering
the other, revealing the naked essence
so caressed and concealed. One yields
to the rocking motion, the pulling gulf
and push of the other. And one receives
the other, as the still depths of a winter
lake receive the revelation of day; and one
knows forever the one entered, as a silver

spasm of rain knows forever the river
it penetrates.

Lungs can take in neither water
nor light. I wonder how it would be
to drown slowly in water and light, yet live,
to know the body swift and seamless
as water, to see the bones as divergent
and willing as light, to recognize in death
the lift of water, the taste of light.

At night, when one watches starlight rise
through water, up from the deepest black
rock crevices and caves at the bottom
of a canyon lake, it might be possible
to forget any concept of surfaces, any fixed
orientation of heaven, to love immediately
the inseparable differences between
the dark soul of water, the thirsting
redemption of light.

Into the Light

There may be some places the sun
never reaches—into the stamen
of a prairie primrose bud burned
and withered before blooming,
or into the eyes of a fetal
lamb killed before born. I suppose
the sun could never shine by its own
light back beyond the moment
when it first congealed and ignited.

And Mohammed, it is said, never showed
the inside of his mouth.

But the sun is certainly present
in the black below the earth, shining
inside the surf and thriving minerals
of sycamore, beech and hickory roots.
Blind fishes at the perpetually sunless
sea bottom hold some daylight in their bodies
by the descending crab particles
and plankton crumbs they sift
through and swallow.

The sun of ten million years previous
stabs and glimmers still in the suspended
beat of glacial bacteria, in salt
crystals frozen beneath miles of ice,
a discernible history of light.

Sun off sunflowers gone
for a hundred years is yet here today
in paint on canvas, just as the radiance

of summer trout watched by Schubert
is the sound of sun now in notes
printed on a staff.

And the sun may shine inside a rock
buried on the dark side of the moon,
if I imagine it there. It might illuminate
the buried night existing inside a dead
man's heart, if I say it is so.

If I envision it, could the sun,
shining maybe at first only faintly
like a penny candle or with a light dim
as the light of the Weaver Star, reveal
the outlines of descending salvation
in an icy rain falling at midnight
through a still forest, the black edges
of atonement in the wooden blades
of the desert saltbush? I close
my eyes and turn in that direction
to see.

The Eye Has No Will of Its Own

It can only follow wherever
the bank swallow leads it over the sandbar
willow upstream, above the little walnut,
the eye bound to the swallow-gyre,
the swallow-fall-and-sweep.

The eye perusing a yellow locust tree
must turn exactly in the way each pod
has turned. It has always had to move straight
without deviation in order to divine
a streak of slanted sun through forest smoke.

The eye increases when the giant green
anemone spreads, when the ash wings
of the flycatcher open. It must stay still
when the hawk moth it studies is stopped.
An orange banner in a wind, the torn frills
of bull kelp in a surf—both control it
with fluttering currents and curls.

Easily coerced to spirals by the conch
and the periwinkle, it is taken in circles
by a balsam leaf in a whirlpool. It is carried
away suddenly past hedges of ligustrum,
then abandoned, then compelled again upward
to the evening sky, by the whims
of a firefly.

What else can it do to find the form
of the seaside arrowgrasses except submit
to their constant collapse and rolling
resurrections? The marbled spider

descends at dusk on its sun-thin tether.
The eye, attendant, becomes one
with the pace of eight-legged descent.

The eye might shut itself, close
itself according to its own choice.
But then, behind that blind, it can only
re-envision all the many-toed tints
and fumbles, the past pacings, the flaring
pauses, all the manipulations and multiple
dictators of its previously fabricated soul.

Cause and Effect, Far and Aware

When the flagfish swerved in the sea,
spread her crippled wings and lifted
toward the wavering green water
of the submerged sun, Lena shifted,
turned in the weightlessness of her sleep,
pressed her belly to the bed
as if the dawn light were rising
beneath the sheet and ticking, up
through the springs and the boards
of the floor.

The running of the bells announcing
a new baby boy born living in May
caused a thousand buds of the prairie solstice
to push themselves forward into blossoms,
thus making a thousand new worlds
for starlight, for cricket pluckings,
for moonsome coyote quarrels to shine upon.

And when Robert put his lips with love
to the breast of a woman for the first time,
a scarcely perceptible glimmer of violet
widened briefly on the corona arc
of Stellar Maris, then thinned
and fell again as he rose.

The moment after the pod of the *yucca baccata*
broke, spilling a scatter of seeds unseen
against the rocky grasslands, a similar
scatter of northern blue butterflies hovered
unwitnessed over a shallow of mud-dampness,
became a pattern of drift against the evening

crowberry and laurel, a chord hanging
like scattered notes against the ear
of the deaf.

What happened yesterday—a subtle
movement of molecules? a strum or less
of electrons?—that caused the surf to curl
its lather a thread farther up the steel clay
beach, that caused the bend and grip
of the bumblebee to hasten in the building
of her honey pots, that urged the cloudy
salamander to stretch beneath the talus
debris one minute longer?

If the red-legged frog, gorgeous *rana aurora,*
will simply blink the bronze of its eye
once more quickly, maybe I can watch
and measure what thunder misses a beat
in the poplar's heartwood, assess what future
fire of vision in the artist's hand
is gathering, glimpse by glimpse,
toward combustion.

Design of Gongs

Each single spill of rain makes
many ringing water gongs on the pond,
and the calls of the crow are simply one gong
sounding after the other, circling wider
and farther, rippling the sky
above the rippled pond.

Below, a toad bug swivels near the shore,
and many sand grains shiver like cymbals
with the force of that mallet.

The bordering red clover is a gong too,
the way its ruby light spreads, stuns
and echoes in the eye, and the cowpen
daisy—those bold rays of reverberations
fly on and on, clear back to the sun.

The turning wind makes of every quaking
poplar leaf a gong. What a constant
confetti of green percussion that ensemble
of summer aspen creates on the bluff.
Coyote sirens and calls interstice
wildly, override, merge, shrieking,
shaking this entire whining and weaving
design of gongs.

Breathe, breathe. Now the tremblings
and drummings of the early moon spread
through the tambourine thistles, swirl
the bee and beetle dust of the evening,
sizzle the whole heavens and zing
until all crystals of every sense

are struck and dizzy with its continual
white shammerings.

Far away an electron at the edge
of a Sanctus is startled, twirled and redefined
by the solstice gong of the orbiting
earth announcing the first new prayer
of the next season.

The Long Marriage: A Translation

In among the alder's highest black
branches making a complicated map
of depth and elevation against the dull
white sky, winter waxwings in a flock
settle, coming, going.

They depart, altering the design of cold
and season in the tree, return
in gatherings of six or seven, flying
in quick staccato against a largo
of motion relative to one another,
as if they weren't birds alone
but a constantly changing syntax
in a history of place and event.

Several sail together over the fallen
field with an expansion and contraction
of pattern that might sound like a wheezing
of wooden organ or bagpipe, were there sound
to vision. And eleven spiral up, angle
into the evening like eleven dead leaves
with stunted wings and no more purpose
nor will than to illustrate eleven
different motives of the wind at once.

Gliding to gully, to river brush, a wave
of them parts easily, rejoins in crossing
familiarities that might impress like lavender
and sage, were there fragrances
to involution and grace.

Back and forth in ragged unison
through the network of branches, penetrating

and teetering, they leave the dense
scaffolding like torn pieces of broken tree
and veer toward the east; they return
from the west to circle and descend
again into the bare limbs of the alder
back in its place once more. Swerving
and sinking through the light,
they are a hard statement of fact
ameliorating itself midair.

I know evening and alder and waxwings
to one another can never be fixed. No constant
coordinate ever contains them. The new amber
of the sky moves toward darkness. Branches
and birds change places continuously,
as if definition also possessed no certain
form heightening and fading. Night stars,
invisible behind the hour, are bright
in the imagination, silent
with shifting prophecy.

Creation, by Season,
of the Very First Desire

Deep inside the spore-sphere
of a protozoa rising slowly
through cold lulls and currents, blue

with a blue like the under-figment
of early spring waterweed in shadow,

rising in burst and dalliance
past the lurch of a carp's flat
eye, past the fast black trills
of filament-tails in eggs floating

beneath dormant river cress, falling
upward in stutter and eloquence,
drifting netherside up in die

and demand, surrounded by many
flattering wheels circling sideways
toward moon, lapsing, pushing toward sun,

deep inside the spore-sphere
of a protozoa, a small fledge of heat
is asking, in a repetition of the very
first cry and reverie known on earth,
for summer.

Investigative Logic in a Study of Love

The field, persistent in its meticulous
study of lantern flies, leaf hoppers, elbowed
antennae and the lightning of sperm,
is the love of the sky made flesh.

To properly study love then,
the sky must be carefully observed
in the act of becoming a curve of yellow clover
or the mouth of an io moth.

The study of the panicled aster and the tent
of the shamrock spider is the invisible love
of the field given sight. Therefore, any fondness
for the rooting of skies can first be seen
in the close examination of Indian grass,
timothy and autumn bluestem alive in the field.

The study of the burrowing habits of the speckled
tortoise, carried out with solicitude,
is obviously an alternative investigation
of the rituals of sky-worship, and the touching
and naming of prairie flower and brush-footed
butterfly is either love studying itself
or the field revealing, piece by piece, the love
of the sky or the love of the mind recognized
as itself through blossom and wing.

The sky has already discovered the white-tailed kite
as the airborne love of such a field study.

The inevitable conclusion is
that the thoroughly studied field will certainly shine

forever afterwards, on its own, like love.
I tell you it will give forth light like the sky
and reflect in all directions like the mind cherishing
the studious glory of a seeded dandelion scattering
its brilliant wind of stars before the sun.

The Way I'm Taught by Heart

The way I'm taught how to move
my hand along the swelve
and lank of your naked back
is by having watched how a pine
in easy wind smooths itself along
the close spine of a summer
night. The way I know how to drink
at your mouth is by remembering
my mouth at the earth once
taking sweet spring water
with my eyes closed.

I learn how to speak to you now
by imitating the cholla blossoms
who, in their hour, speak of lust
and expiation, and I seek you
in the same way the marblewings
opening in dampness at dawn admit
for their own edification every last
probe of sun possible.

Rising and falling inside your arms,
I understand how mosses and cress lose
and gain over and over inside the hold
of a stream. I've seen the headlong
push forward of a trout nudging
upcreek in a current.

Deep sea geographies of spiraling
canyons and cols, sudden stellar-scatters
and the chances beyond—these are the same words
as the words of your body, your name,

as I pronounce it, identical to wind-borne
riflings of rain above desert light.

Here I am, like God, the pulsing
center in a gather of waxwings widening
and tightening in their flock against
the sky, like God, a wayward thread
of cottonwood lifting over fields,
forswearing forever all bones,
every place.

Egg

Perhaps the light inside this temple
is less than a small candle barely
burning beneath a violet shade,
an uncertain diffusion like a glow
of glacier at night without moon,
a presence like morning over a pale
field before dawn, dimmer than day
with no voice to declare it.

Were there ears to hear inside
these halls, then a constant connecting
like scales of organ chords played
in arpeggio by two hands might be heard
as the spine assembles itself, a sound
like the low pizzicato of a cello
as the first faint plicking
of pulse commences.

One could claim a belief in crosses
exists predestined in the pattern
of arteries forming their junctures
yet to appear.

Were a seer present she might say
the attention inside this temple
is like that of rock spurs suddenly
quaked and rebounded by lightning.

Were a shaman present inside
these translucent walls, he might say
the sentiment is like that in a random

meadow of columbine filled
with mountain air before rain.

And were a master in the making here,
he might claim the process witnessed
in the rising and joining of warm wax
cells and oils is god, the exquisite
weaving of salt ropes and red twines
is the presence of god.

Though not one single star
exists in the curved breadth
of this structure, yet the only possible
place where any star might be found
is inside the immeasurable horizon
of the thin-skulled cranium about to be.

Could it be a worship of any kind
beheld in this first absence moving
toward a possible breath of protest
and sacrament?

When the last latching occurs, bringing
the rude kick and the cry, then this temple
must fail, fall, shatter away altogether,
and the world, at once, begin anew.

H. EMERSON BLAKE

PATTIANN ROGERS has published six books of poetry: *The Expectations of Light* (Princeton, 1981), *The Tattooed Lady in the Garden* (Wesleyan, 1986), *Legendary Performance* (Ion Press, 1987), *Splitting and Binding* (Wesleyan, 1989), *Geocentric* (Gibbs Smith, 1993), and *Firekeeper: New and Selected Poems* (Milkweed, 1994). She has been the recipient of two NEA grants, a Guggenheim Fellowship, and a Lannan Poetry Fellowship. Her poems have won several prizes, including the Tietjens Prize and the Hokin Prize from *Poetry,* the Roethke Prize from *Poetry Northwest,* the Strousse Award twice from *Prairie Schooner,* three book awards from the Texas Institute of Letters, and four Pushcart Prizes. She is a graduate of the University of Missouri (B.A.) and the University of Houston (M.A.) and has been a visiting writer at the University of Texas, the University of Montana, and the University of Arkansas and a member of the faculty of Vermont College. The mother of two grown sons, Pattiann Rogers lives with her husband, a geophysicist, in Colorado.

ACKNOWLEDGMENTS

My thanks to the editors of the following magazines in which these poems first appeared.

Alaska Quarterly: "Service with Benediction," originally titled "Eating Bread and Honey (Service with Benediction)."

Amicus: "Opus from Space"; "The Kingdom of Heaven"; "Into the Light."

Fine Madness: "Within One Moment, All Possible Moments"; "Creation, by Season, of the Very First Desire."

Georgia Review: "Egg"; "Of Possibility: Another Autumn Leaving."

Gettysburg Review: "Murder in the Good Land"; "Kaleidoscope: Free Will and the Nature of the Holy Spirit"; "'God Is in the Details,' Says Mathematician Freeman J. Dyson."

High Fantastic: "The Death of Living Rocks and the Consequences Thereof."

Hudson Review: "The Consequences of Death."

Iowa Review: "Creation by the Presence of Absence: City Coyote in Rain"; "Abundance and Satisfaction"; "The Way I'm Taught by Heart."

Interdisciplinary Studies in Literature and the Environment: "The Eye Has No Will of Its Own"; "Going for Water and Light."

Kenyon Review: "Where Do Your People Come From?"; "Mousefeet: From a Lecture on Muridae Cosmology."

Orion: "Animals and People: 'The Human Heart in Conflict with Itself.'"

Paris Review: "The Singing Place"; "The Fallacy of Thinking Flesh Is Flesh"; "The Art of Raising Gibbons and Flowers."

Plum Review: "Kissing a Kit Fox"; "Orange Thicket: To Speak in Tongues."

Poetry: "Nearing Autobiography"; "Rapture of the Deep: The Pattern of Poseidon's Love Song"; "Design of Gongs"; "Investigative Logic in a Study of Love."

Poetry Northwest: "Partners"; "Remembering the Present Tense"; "The Immortal Soul."

Prairie Schooner: "The Long Marriage: A Translation"; "Against the Ethereal"; "The Center of the Known Universe."

Quarterly West Review: "Inside the Universe Inside the Act"; "Place and Proximity"; "Fractal: Repetition of Form over a Variety of Scales."

Talking River Review: "Cause and Effect, Far and Aware."

"Abundance and Satisfaction" appears in *The Best American Poetry, 1996,* edited by Adrienne Rich and published by Scribner.

"The Long Marriage: A Translation," "Against the Ethereal," and "The Center of the Known Universe" were given the 1996 Strousse Award from *Prairie Schooner.*

"Nearing Autobiography" appears in the *1995/1996 Anthology of Magazine Verse and Yearbook of American Poetry.*

Interior design by Will Powers.
Typeset in Legacy Serif
by Stanton Publication Services, Inc.
Printed on acid-free Booktext Natural paper
by BookCrafters.

Passages North Anthology:
A Decade of Good Writing
Edited by Elinor Benedict

Civil Blood
Jill Breckenridge

Drive, They Said:
Poems about Americans and Their Cars
Edited by Kurt Brown

Night Out:
Poems about Hotels, Motels, Restaurants, and Bars
Edited by Kurt Brown and Laure-Anne Bosselaar

Astonishing World:
Selected Poems of Ángel González
Translated from the Spanish by Steven Ford Brown

Mixed Voices:
Contemporary Poems about Music
Edited by Emilie Buchwald and Ruth Roston

The Poet Dreaming in the Artist's House:
Contemporary Poems about the Visual Arts
Edited by Emilie Buchwald and Ruth Roston

This Sporting Life:
Contemporary American Poems about Sports and Games
Edited by Emilie Buchwald and Ruth Roston

The Art of Writing:
Lu Chi's Wen Fu
Translated from the Chinese by Sam Hamill

In a Sheep's Eye, Darling
Margaret Hasse

Trusting Your Life to Water and Eternity:
Twenty Poems by Olav H. Hauge
Translated from the Norwegian
by Robert Bly

Boxelder Bug Variations
Bill Holm

The Dead Get By with Everything
Bill Holm

This Error is the Sign of Love
Lewis Hyde

Looking for Home:
Women Writing about Exile
Edited by Deborah Keenan and Roseann Lloyd

The Freedom of History
Jim Moore

The Long Experience of Love
Jim Moore

Minnesota Writes:
Poetry
Edited by Jim Moore and Cary Waterman